REACH OUT YOUTH SOLUTIONS
WWW.REACH-OUT.ORG

Parent Fuel Journal
Copyright © 2007 by Barry St. Clair
Published by Reach Out Youth Solutions
        www.reach-out.org <http://www.reach-out.org/>
        1 (800) 473-9456
        1505 Lilburn-Stone Mountain Rd #235
        Stone Mountain, GA 30087

All rights reserved. No part of this publication may be reproduced, stored in a retrieval system or transmitted in any form by any means, electronic, mechanical, photocopy, recording or otherwise, without the prior permission of the publisher, except as provided for by USA copyright law.

Cover design: Josh Dennis

Cover illustration: Leonello Calvetti

First printing, 2007

Printed in the United States of America

ISBN 13:   978-1-931617-30-7

Unless otherwise indicated, Scripture quotations are taken from *The Holy Bible: New International Version*®. Copyright © 1973, 1978, 1984 by International Bible Society. Used by permission of Zondervan Publishing House. All rights reserved. The "NIV" and "New International Version" trademarks are registered in the United States Patent and Trademark Office by International Bible Society. Use of either trademark requires the permission of International Bible Society.

Bible quotations indicated as from KJV are taken from *The Holy Bible: King James Version*.

Bible quotations from *The Message*, copyright © 1993, 1994, 1995, 1996, 2000, 2001, 2002 by Eugene H. Peterson, are used by permission.

Bible quotations indicated as from RSV are taken from *The Holy Bible: Revised Standard Version*, copyright © 1946, 1971 by Division of Christian Education of the National Council of Churches of Christ in the United States of America. Used by permission.

18	17	16	15	14	13	12	11	10	09	08	07
15	14	13	12	11	10	9	8	7	6	5	4	3	2	1

Contents

Introduction   6

Fuel the Fire First in Us

1. Wanted: Fire-Builders—Perfection Not Required for This Job   9
   How do we break through our imperfections to pursue God's purpose for our kids?
2. Stoke the Spark—From God to Parents to Kids   17
   How do we connect with God's primary desire for us and our kids?
3. Dry Out the Firewood: Gain New Purpose for Old Pain   25
   How do we find healing for our hurts to avoid passing those hurts to our children?
4. Dry More Firewood: Gain More New Purpose for Old Pain   33
   How do we follow through on our healing to avoid imposing pain on our children?
5. Create a Draft: Open the Door and Let Grace Blow In   41
   How do we rely on God's resources to raise our kids?

Kindle a Warm Relationship with Our Kids

6. Stir Up the Fire by Relating to Our Kids   49
   How do we connect with a disconnected generation?
7. Burn Away the Junk to Find the Heart of Gold   57
   How do we help our children discover their hearts?
8. Build a Fire That Blazes with Intimacy   65
   How do we love our kids unconditionally?
9. Feed the Fire with Communication   73
   How do we communicate positively with our kids?
10. Pour Fuel on the Fire by Making Disciples   81
    How do we invest in Jesus-focused relationships with our kids and their friends?

Spread a Wildfire In and Through Our Kids

11. Fan the Flame with Discipline   89
    How do we equip our children to move from dependence to independence?
12. Intensify the Heat with Destiny   97
    How do we inspire our kids to discover their unique direction in life?
13. Don't Let Disappointment Douse the Fire   105
    How do we build our children's confidence in God when life lets them down?
14. Glow in the Light of God's Vision   113
    How do we motivate our kids to pursue God's dream for their lives?
15. Spread the Fire of God's Desire   121
    How do we release our children to change the world?

PARENT FUEL KIT

FOR YOU, YOUR FAMILY, YOUR CHURCH AND SMALL GROUP

The **Parent Fuel Kit** by Barry St. Clair has more fuel for your parenting fire!

Parent Fuel. This book equips parents to fuel a fire for Christ in the hearts of your kids. It offers a fresh perspective for relating to and investing in your children.

Parent Fuel Journal. This companion piece to the **Parent Fuel** book gives you the tools to reflect further on your parenting and on your kids and then to implement the practical realities of the book.

Parent Fuel Audio CDs. Presented live before parents, these talks offer encouragement and guidance from Barry's parenting experience.

Parent Fuel DVD Series. This six-session highly interactive DVD series inspires and motivates. It features Barry St. Clair and a variety of parents expressing their struggles and successes in parenting their kids, along with time for small group discussion. These fifty-five minute videos enhance the message of the **Parent Fuel** book to parents in your church, small group, school or neighborhood.

Parent Fuel Leader's Guide is included in the kit.

TO ORDER: WWW.SHOPREACHOUT.COM OR (800) 473-9456

To discover how to receive training that will bring the Parent Fuel Experience to your church or small group, go to **www.reach-out.org**

Love the Lord your God with all your heart
and with all your soul and with all your mind.
This is the first and greatest commandment.

JESUS

I WANT TO BE JUST LIKE YOU

Lord, I want to be just like You
'Cause he wants to be just like me
I want to be a holy example
For his innocent eyes to see
Help me be a living Bible, Lord
That my little boy can read
I want to be just like You
'Cause he wants to be like me.

(Phillips, Craig and Dean song "I Want To Be Just Like You")
Used with Permission

PARENT FUEL JOURNAL

How Can This Journal Help You?

The Journal you hold in your hand is added fuel. More fuel causes the fire to increase in intensity and size. As you complete the *Parent Fuel* book, the CDs and this Journal, you will have extra fuel. With that mega-fuel you will discover how to guide your children to passionately pursue Jesus, and in the process they will discover their hearts. Once the fire starts, it spreads quickly. God ignites the spark; we pour the fuel on the spark in their hearts; the spark turns into a blaze; and then their brightly burning fire spreads to others. In a word, you will FUEL THE FIRE IN YOUR CHILD'S HEART!

Only one group of parents can benefit from this Journal: imperfect parents. If you have mastered parenting, you can pass on this Journal. But if you find yourself with uncertainty, doubts, fears and questions, then the extra fuel in your hand is for you!

Neither the book nor this Journal gives you lists of "do's and don'ts." You will not find a formula for producing "godly children." Instead, you will learn that, when you offer your children the opportunity to discover God's love for them through you, they will be motivated from their hearts. That motivation will fuel their passion for Jesus, which will change their thinking and attitudes. That, in turn, will impact their decisions. And, their decisions will drive their behavior. In other words, their behavior will flow from a passionate heart on fire for Jesus Christ.

The Reason for the Journal

This Journal provides you with a companion piece to the book and CDs. Going through this Journal…

- gives you added motivation to implement what you discovered in the book.
- provides you with a specific place to record your insights about your parenting and your children's growth and development.
- offers you a specific opportunity to pray for your children daily.
- makes available a place for you to keep on journaling AFTER you read the book.

The Benefits of the Journal

By going through the Journal, several important benefits will emerge that will result in a sharper focus and greater insight into your parenting style and your children's motivation.

- Reviewing the book will lead you into a deeper understanding of what you read.
- Pondering your parenting will change the way you handle your children.
- Reflecting on your children's lives will help you identify what is in their hearts.
- Journaling with your spouse will lead to a closer relationship between you and more togetherness in your parenting approach.
- Praying for your children will connect you closer to God and to your children.
- Taking suggested steps of action will result in specific changes both to your parenting style and to a greater awareness of your children's needs.
- Reading further in the resources will give you even more parenting fuel for the fire.

When all is said and done, your children will have a greater passion for Jesus kindled by their relationship with you.

PARENT FUEL JOURNAL

How Do You Max Out This Journal?

In this Journal each chapter will lead you to reflect purposefully on your parenting and your children through a variety of elements. By going through this process, God will speak to you and guide you into His insights and actions for you and for your children.

To max out this Journal, CARVE OUT TIME DAILY! Schedule fifteen to thirty minutes each day to reflect, write, memorize, pray and take steps of action. Each chapter is designed to help you accomplish that.

- Pray the **Prayer to Begin** at the beginning of the chapter—pray aloud if you like.
- Read and reflect on the **Thought for Reflection.**
- Give a **Quick Response** to what you read in the corresponding chapter of the book.
- Pray through **My Daily Parenting Prayers**. Pray one prayer each day.
- Memorize the **Verse to Remember**. Go over it daily.
- Answer the **Penetrating Questions** by recording your personal and parenting reflections on what God is saying to you about the topic of that chapter. (These match the Penetrating Questions at the end of each chapter of the book.) Try to answer one Penetrating Question each day.
- Use the **Taking Action** page to write the steps of action that God shows you. (These match the Taking Action section at the end of each chapter of the book.) Work on your Taking Action plans a little each day.
- Think creatively about how you can use one of the **Fresh Ideas**. (These match the Fresh Ideas in the book.)
- Look at the **Further Reading** section to find more resources on the topic of the chapter. Ordering and studying these resources can further enhance your parenting skills.

Now, before you begin, take time to pray Ask God's Spirit to fill you with His thoughts about your parenting and about your children. Ask Him to minimize the distractions so you can focus on Him. Ask Him to use the book and this Journal to build a roaring fire for Christ in your kids!

Wanted: Fire-Builders—
Perfection Not Required for This Job

*How do we break through our imperfections
to pursue God's purpose for our kids?*

PARENT FUEL JOURNAL

 Prayer to Begin

Jesus, I admit that I am not a perfect parent.

 Thought for Reflection

All of us are imperfect parents. Even though we are inadequate in ourselves, God has called us to be parents. It is a holy calling!

Quick Response

Briefly jot down your insights, thoughts and emotions after reading this chapter of the book.

 Verse to Memorize

Do not put out the Spirit's fire. (1 Thessalonians 5:19)

My Daily Parenting Prayers

Pray one of these prayers each day and then write any other prayers or thoughts that the Lord brings to your mind.

Sunday

Lord, show me my imperfections. Allow me to be honest as I face my personal and parenting flaws.

Monday

Jesus, when my parenting imperfections tend to paralyze me, remove the darkness and confusion.

Tuesday

Holy Spirit, release me from the things I could have done differently. Hound of Heaven, woo my children back to You.

Wednesday

Father, make up for the times when my children needed more from me than I gave them. Let me see that with You, it is never too late.

Thursday

Counselor, protect me from comparing myself to others. Guide me to pursue my self-worth not in my kids, but rather in You Who offers real security.

Friday

Jesus, to You I give my guilt over wrong parenting decisions I have made. I accept Your forgiveness now. Cover those mistakes with Your love.

Saturday

Father, You have called me to be a parent. Ignite a fire in me for You and kindle a passion for Christ in my kids.

Penetrating Questions

Breaking through your imperfections will lead you toward pursuing God's purpose for your kids. Reflecting on these questions will help you deal practically with those imperfections.

1. On a scale of 1-10 how easy is it for you to admit that you are an imperfect parent?

2. What one example can you give of your imperfection with your children?

3. What one example can you offer of your children's imperfections? (Name only one.)

4. Which "black hole" do you tend to fall into most often? Why?

5. How do you think God wants to get you out, keep you out, and move you beyond that black hole?

6. In spite of your imperfections, what purpose does God have for you as a parent?

7. How do you see yourself fueling a passion for Christ in your kids?

Taking Action

Think about which "black hole" you tend to fall into. Ask God to show you why and how you have fallen into that hole. Ask Him to show you how to get out. Write down what you discover.

 **Thought for Reflection**

God and His love for you prevail over your imperfections.

Fresh Ideas

Read the "Fresh Ideas" and use one of them to help you work through your imperfections so you can pursue God's purpose for your parenting. Place a ✔ by the one you choose and then record your thoughts on how you want to use it.

- Viewing yourself positively, not negatively, provides one of the fastest ways to create fresh ideas about your parenting. That positive view of yourself will begin to emerge after you admit your imperfections. Write down your parenting imperfections.

- After deciding which black hole you fall into most often, ask God to show you a specific plan to get out and stay out. Write out the plan.

- In a phrase that will fit on a T-shirt, write out your parenting purpose, then have it painted onto a T-shirt or some other surface. Display your purpose some place where you will see it regularly.

- Share with your spouse what you have written above. Pray for each other about the parenting black holes you fall into and about your parenting purpose. Appropriately communicate the same to your children.

 ## Further Reading

Brent Curtis and John Eldredge, *The Sacred Romance* (Nashville: Thomas Nelson, 1997). This book will allow you to see your imperfections against the story of God's love for you. It will help you see how you fit into God's story in spite of your flaws and failures.

Tim Kimmel, *Grace-Based Parenting* (Nashville: W Publishing Group, 2004). This book offers grace and truth, love and purpose, as well as hope and freedom for your parenting adventure.

PARENT FUEL JOURNAL

My Personal and Parenting Reflections

Use this space to record your insights, thoughts, emotions, hopes and dreams for yourself, your family and for each of your children.

For Myself:

For Our Family:

For My Children:

Stoke the Spark—
From God to Parents to Kids

How do we connect with God's primary desire for us and our kids?

PARENT FUEL JOURNAL

 Prayer to Begin

Jesus, place inside of me the passion to love You with all of my heart, soul, mind and strength and to lead my children to love You like I do.

 Thought for Reflection

Our kids will passionately pursue what they see us passionately pursue!

 Quick Response

Briefly jot down your insights, thoughts and emotions after reading this chapter of the book.

 Verse to Memorize

Hear, O Israel: The Lord our God, the Lord is one. Love the Lord your God with all your heart and with all your soul, and with all your strength. These commandments that I give you today are to be upon your hearts. Impress them on your children. (Deuteronomy 6:5-7a)

2. My Daily Parenting Prayers

Pray one of these prayers each day and then write any other prayers or thoughts that the Lord brings to your mind.

Sunday

Lord, I repeat Your words to You as my prayer: I desire to love the Lord my God with all my heart and with all my soul, and with all my strength.

Monday

God, show me how I can help my children love Jesus more.

Tuesday

Jesus, I know that following You is "more caught than taught" and that my kids will probably be passionate about what I am passionate about. Make me more passionate about You.

Wednesday

Father, show me anything that dampens Your flame inside of me. Let me see how my passions motivate my kids to come toward You or de-motivate them causing them to move away from You.

Thursday

Holy Spirit, give me the courage to put You in the "black box" of my life daily.

Friday

Lord, I bring all of my decisions and our family's decisions to the "kitchen table" now. (Make a list of those decisions.)

Saturday

Lord, let me love You with such authenticity and enthusiasm that my kids are surrounded by You every place they touch my life. Let Your love pass from my heart to my kids' hearts.

PARENT FUEL JOURNAL

❓ *Penetrating Questions*

A heart wide open to God—honest, available, tender, seeking—cannot be hidden from our children. Reflecting on these questions will help you discover how your heart can be like that.

1. What primary desire does God have for parents and through parents to kids?

2. In what ways have you leaned your ladder against the wrong wall of "How do I make my children turn out right?"

3. In what ways have you leaned your ladder against the right wall of "How do I help my children love Jesus more?"

4. If "Love God" expresses the one clear message God has for you and your children, how do you see that working out with you and with your children?

5. How has the spark of love for God gotten doused? How do you think God wants to renew the spark?

6. Is Jesus in the "black box" of your life? What difference has that decision made for you and for your children?

7. Does Jesus sit at the head of the table in your home? What difference has that made for you and for your children?

 **Taking Action**

Answer the question: *Do I love God with all my heart?*

If not, write down the reasons why and the consequences that has brought into your life and into your children's lives. Since there is no time like the present, write out your statement to God telling Him that you want to decide now to put Him in the "black box" of your life and place Him at the head of your family table.

If you do love God with all your heart, write the value and consequences of that decision in your life and in your children's lives.

 **Thought for Reflection**

God's love passes from our hearts to their hearts.

Fresh Ideas

Read the "Fresh Ideas" and use one of them to enhance God's primary desire for you and your kids. Place a ✔ by the one you choose and then record your thoughts on how you want to use it.

- Note your interactions with your kids this week, and give attention to which conversations focused on behavior and which ones focused on the heart.

- Memorize Matthew 22:37-38.

- To daily remind you to connect with God's primary desire for you and your kids, write "Love God" on one side of a piece of paper and "Jesus" on the other side. Put it in a black box or, if you prefer, in your wallet, on your dashboard or on your computer screen.

- Realize that if you love Jesus, your kids benefit by hanging around you. Put on your calendar specifically when you will spend time with your kids this week.

- Around your kitchen table (or your special place to meet in your house) write personal and family concerns on a card. Pray about one of those concerns each night at dinner.

 Further Reading

John Eldredge, *Wild at Heart* (Nashville: Thomas Nelson, 2001). Dads who want to passionately pursue God will love this book!

John Piper, *Don't Waste Your Life* (Wheaton, IL: Crossway Books, 2003). This book will challenge you to further explore your highest purpose.

PARENT FUEL JOURNAL

My Personal and Parenting Reflections

Use this space to record your insights, thoughts, emotions, hopes and dreams for yourself, your family and for each of your children.

For Myself:

For Our Family:

For My Children:

Dry Out the Firewood:
Gain New Purpose for Old Pain

*How do we find healing for our hurts
without passing those hurts to our children?*

 **Prayer to Begin**

Father of Mercies, comfort me in my pain. Let me see where I have been hurt by my parents and/or other people. You are the Wounded Healer. I know that You are the only One who can bring healing to me. Help me to face my wounds honestly.

 Thought for Reflection

The people who hurt us most are often those closest to us.

 Quick Response

Briefly jot down your insights, thoughts and emotions after reading this chapter of the book.

 Verse to Memorize

The punishment that brought us peace was upon him, and by his wounds we are healed. (Isaiah 53: 5b)

My Daily Parenting Prayers

Pray one of these prayers each day and then write any other prayers or thoughts that the Lord brings to your mind.

Sunday

Father of Mercies, show me how my parents have inflicted pain on me and how that has impacted my life.

Monday

Jesus, thank You that You have experienced all of my pain ahead of me.

Tuesday

Suffering Servant, let me see the depth of Your woundedness for me.

Wednesday

Comforter, give me courage to face and feel the pain that my parents have caused me.

Thursday

Deliverer, You are the only One who can deliver me from my hurts and tears. Please deliver me.

Friday

Wounded Healer, let me experience Your healing of my wounds.

Saturday

Counselor, do Your work in my life so You can use me to bring healing to my family.

Penetrating Questions

Each of us is the product of our parents and the way they parented us. Some people have experienced their parents positively. Others have experienced them painfully. Reflecting on these questions will help you in a practical way to find healing.

Think about one of these questions each day for the next week.

1. What one major hurt have your parents inflicted on you?

2. What other wounds has your family painfully imposed on you?

3. What do you see as the results of those wounds in your life?

4. What impact have your wounds had on your children?

5. Why do you think Jesus, the Wounded Healer, can heal you? (Review Isaiah 53:2-6.)

6. What specific wounds do you want Him to heal?

7. How do you want to express your healing prayer to the Wounded Healer?

PARENT FUEL JOURNAL

 Taking Action

As you answer the seven "Penetrating Questions," let the Wounded Healer rescue you, heal you and remove your pain.

 Thought for Reflection

In Jesus' suffering He identifies with my suffering. Through Jesus' suffering He heals my hurts.

Dry Out the Firewood: Gain New Purpose for Old Pain

 Fresh Ideas

Read the "Fresh Ideas" and use one of them to assist you in moving from woundedness to wholeness. Place a ✔ by the one you choose and then record your thoughts on how you want to use it.

- Identify any sin that has dominated your extended family. Trace it through your family tree as far back as you can.

- Create a picture of Jesus as portrayed in Isaiah 53:2-6. Then around that picture write the characteristics of the Wounded Healer.

- Then on the back of that paper draw a cross. Around the cross list all the wounds you have experienced, and then write next to each wound how Jesus experienced that same hurt, again referring to Isaiah 53:2-6. With each hurt express how Jesus, the Wounded Healer, wants to heal you.

- Record, in writing, your decision and prayer to let Jesus, the Wounded Healer, heal you.

 Further Reading

Henri Nouwen, *The Wounded Healer* (New York: Image Books, Random House, 1979). Brief, yet profound, this treatise on Jesus as the Wounded Healer gives fuller explanation of Jesus' ability to heal our wounds.

PARENT FUEL JOURNAL

 My Personal and Parenting Reflections

Use this space to record your insights, thoughts, emotions, hopes and dreams for yourself, your family and for each of your children.

For Myself:

For Our Family:

For My Children:

Dry More Firewood:
Gain More New Purpose for Old Pain

*How do we follow through on our healing
to avoid imposing pain on our children?*

Prayer to Begin

Jesus, bring me to the place where I can give and receive forgiveness freely.

 Thought for Reflection

God forgave us without any merit on our part.

 Quick Response

Briefly jot down your insights, thoughts and emotions after reading this chapter of the book.

 Verse to Memorize

For if you forgive men when they sin against you, your heavenly Father will also forgive you. But if you do not forgive men their sins, your Father will not forgive your sins. (Matthew 6:14-15)

My Daily Parenting Prayers

Pray one of these prayers each day and then write any other prayers or thoughts that the Lord brings to your mind.

Sunday

Lord, let me see the value of my precious relationships and have the courage to deal with the conflict involved in those relationships.

Monday

God of All Mercy, I pray for the blood of Jesus to protect and heal my family.

Tuesday

My Shield and Fortress, I pray for Your protection over my family physically, mentally, emotionally and spiritually.

Wednesday

Author of Forgiveness, give me courage to forgive my parents where they have hurt me.

Thursday

Forgiver of All Sin, give me strength to forgive others in my family who have wounded me.

Friday

Father of Mercies, show me how I have wounded my children and give me Your humility to ask for their forgiveness.

Saturday

Counselor, do Your work in my life so You can use me to bring healing to my family.

Penetrating Questions

God wants you to forgive those who have hurt you. Reflecting on these questions will help you practically to give and receive forgiveness. Think about one of these questions each day for the next week.

1. What did your parents do that lowered the value of relationships in your family and kept your relationships from being precious to each other?

2. What does your current family do that lowers the value of relationships and keeps your relationships from being precious to each other?

3. Do you see connections or patterns between questions 1 and 2? What are they?

4. Do you think Satan has gained a foothold in your family? If so, how?

5. How do you need to pray for spiritual protection for your family if in fact Satan does have a foothold?

6. With whom in your family do you have the most conflict? How can the Conflict Curve help you in that relationship?

7. Are you willing to forgive that person? If so, will you walk through the steps of obedience necessary for you to give and receive forgiveness? When will you begin?

PARENT FUEL JOURNAL

 Taking Action

After answering the seven "Penetrating Questions," write down and then take the steps of obedience needed to give and receive forgiveness in order to bring healing to you and to others.

 Thought for Reflection

With those who have hurt you, God wants you to give and receive forgiveness freely.

Dry More Firewood: Gain More New Purpose for Old Pain

 ## *Fresh Ideas*

Read the "Fresh Ideas" and use one of them to assist you in resolving conflict, overcoming strongholds and giving and receiving forgiveness freely. Place a ✔ by the one you choose and then record your thoughts on how you want to use it.

- Write the names of each family member on a piece of paper, both the family in which you grew up and your present family. Identify where each person fits on the Conflict Curve.

- In light of what you discovered from the Conflict Curve about the relationships in your family, list the issues about which you will pray for each person. Divide the sheet in half so you can keep prayers on one side and answers on the other. Pray for these people daily.

- Consider how Satan might have gotten a foothold in your family. Write down what that looks like, and then write a prayer of protection for any or all of the people in your family.

- From your list of family members write the names of any people to whom you need to go and ask forgiveness (see Matthew 5:23-24). Write down what you will say to them. Then, one by one, go and ask forgiveness.

- From that same list write the names of any people who have hurt you, people whom you need to forgive. Write down what you will say when you ask God to help you forgive them.

 ## *Further Reading*

Neil Anderson, *Victory Over the Darkness* (Ventura, CA:, Regal, 2000). In this book you will find more depth and detail on how to give and receive forgiveness.

David Seamands, *Healing for Damaged Emotions* (Wheaton, IL: Victor Books, 1986). This powerful volume offers spiritual insight, excellent illustrations, and practical applications for healing and forgiveness.

PARENT FUEL JOURNAL

 My Personal and Parenting Reflections

Use this space to record your insights, thoughts, emotions, hopes and dreams for yourself, your family and for each of your children.

For Myself:

For Our Family:

For My Children:

Create a Draft:
Open the Door and Let Grace Blow In

How do we rely on God's resources to raise our children?

PARENT FUEL JOURNAL

 Prayer to Begin

God of grace, thank You that You have given me Your grace. It is a gift freely given to me by Jesus Christ. I throw open the door to Your grace and step into it. I close the door on the law, the rules, and my performance. I leave them behind. Let me live my life and parent my children by Your grace.

 Thought for Reflection

And if by grace, then it is no longer by works; if it were, grace would no longer be grace. (The Apostle Paul in Romans 11:6)

 Quick Response

Briefly jot down your insights, thoughts and emotions after reading this chapter of the book.

 Verse to Memorize

But he said, "My grace is sufficient for you for my power is made perfect in weakness". Therefore I will all the more gladly boast about my weaknesses, so that Christ's power may rest on me. (2 Corinthians 12:9)

My Daily Parenting Prayers

Pray one of these prayers each day and then write any other prayers or thoughts that the Lord brings to your mind.

Sunday

God of grace, give me grace to open the door to Your grace.

Monday

Spirit of freedom, free me from any negative influence my parents' rules, expectations of performance or wrong view of success have on me.

Tuesday

Grace Giver, show me how to live by grace.

Wednesday

Lord, I can't. You never said I could. But, Lord, You can. You always said You would.

Thursday

Jesus, show me how to trust You with my children and Your work in my children.

Friday

Holy Spirit, help me ask the question often to my children, "What do you think God is saying to you about that?"

Saturday

Father, fill me with Your Holy Spirit, so that I have Your supernatural ability to raise my children every day.

PARENT FUEL JOURNAL

 Penetrating Questions

God wants us to parent by grace. Reflecting on these questions will help you discover practically how to do that.

1. In your own experience what example illustrates how you have relied on your own parenting skills? What example comes to mind that shows how you relied on God's grace with your children?

2. In your view, how has guilt, fear or performance negatively affected your children?

3. From reading this chapter what has changed in your thinking about internally motivating your kids? About trusting them?

Create a Draft: Open the Door and Let Grace Blow In

4. Will you make the decision to open the grace door for you and your family? What does that decision mean to you?

5. Will you memorize the grace prayer and pray it daily? What difference do you think this prayer will make?

6. When and how will you share the gospel with your children?

7. In what specific situations can you use the question "What do you think God is saying to you about that?" with your children?

PARENT FUEL JOURNAL

 Taking Action

Open the door to God's grace by taking these actions quickly.

1. Decide to open the grace door.
2. Pray the grace prayer daily: Lord, I can't. You never said I could. But, Lord, You can. You always said You would.
3. Share the gospel of grace with each of your children.
4. Appeal to the Holy Spirit in your children. Use the question: What do you think God is saying to you about that?

 Thought for Reflection

Grace: God's supernatural ability in me through the Cross and the Resurrection.

Create a Draft: Open the Door and Let Grace Blow In

 Fresh Ideas

Read the "Fresh Ideas" and use one of them to help you leave the rules behind and open the door to grace. Place a ✔ by the one you choose and then record your thoughts here on how you want to use it.

- Determine the trigger point when guilt, fear or performance traps you personally. Ask the Lord to heal that by His grace.

- Evaluate the trigger point when guilt, fear and performance trap your children. Ask the Healer to heal that also.

- Do a Bible study on grace. Look up all the grace verses in a concordance. Read one at each evening meal. Then ask each person to express thanks for ways they have seen God's grace expressed.

- Gather the material needed, and prepare yourself to share the gospel with your kids.

- Try using the "What do you think God is saying to you about that?" question in a variety of nonthreatening situations with your kids.

 Further Reading

The Good News Glove, a Campus Crusade for Christ tract for leading your child to Christ; www.c cci.org/good-news/index.html. Or contact Reach Out Youth Solutions, www.reach-out.org, for material to lead your teenager to Christ.

Philip Yancey, *What's So Amazing About Grace?* (Grand Rapids, MI: Zondervan, 1997). This excellent book will expand your understanding of grace and broaden your view of how it works.

PARENT FUEL JOURNAL

 My Personal and Parenting Reflections

Use this space to record your insights, thoughts, emotions, hopes and dreams for yourself, your family and for each of your children.

For Myself:

For Our Family:

For My Children:

Stir Up the Fire by Relating to Our Kids

How do we do we connect with a disconnected generation?

PARENT FUEL JOURNAL

 Prayer to Begin

Lord Jesus, make me a bridge. Give me the vision and courage to connect God with my kids and my kids with God.

 Thought for Reflection

To connect God with our kids and our kids with God creates the ultimate bridge of influence!

 Quick Response

Briefly jot down your insights, thoughts and emotions after reading this chapter of the book.

 Verse to Memorize

And David shepherded them with integrity of heart; and with skillful hands he led them. (Psalm 78:72)

My Daily Parenting Prayers

Pray one of these prayers each day and then write any other prayers or thoughts that the Lord brings to your mind.

Sunday

Jesus, You are the ultimate Bridge. Use me as Your bridge of influence to connect You with my kids and my kids with You.

Monday

Lord, You are the Good Shepherd. Prepare me to shepherd my kids with integrity of heart and to lead them with skillful hands.

Tuesday

Protector, Father and Head of the Church, let me see where the culture is destroying my kids, where I have abandoned them and where my church struggles to be relevant to them. Use me to protect them, to relate to them and to find out how to make church relevant to them.

Wednesday

You Who Searches Hearts, give me faith to see that, no matter how outward appearances look, in my kids' hearts they are searching for You.

Thursday

God of Power, show me how I can lead my kids to experience Your dynamic, supernatural power.

Friday

Word of God, confirm to me how I can teach my kids the Word of God so it becomes active and alive to them.

Saturday

Disciple-maker, let me see Your plan to pass on my passionate faith to my kids through disciple-making.

Penetrating Questions

Parents influence their children by becoming a relational bridge that connects God to their kids and their kids to God. Reflecting on these questions will help you discover practically how to become that bridge.

1. What do you think influence is?

2. What factors in the culture, your family and your church contribute to the disconnection with your kids?

3. What can you do specifically to minimize those negative influences that disconnect?

4. In what ways do you see your children searching for God?

5. Do you see yourself as the primary influence in your children's lives? Why? Why not?

6. Will you take on the influential role of a bridge by connecting God to your kids and your kids to God? How do you see yourself doing that?

7. What did you discover from Psalm 78 that has been hidden, but now you see? From those discoveries will you make the decision to show your kids the power of God and the authority of the Word of God by meeting with them to pass on a passionate faith? If so, how do you think that might look?

PARENT FUEL JOURNAL

 Taking Action

Gather the thoughts you discovered in this chapter about connecting with your kids. Then pray about and decide what God wants you to do to become the bridge that connects God to your kids and your kids to God. Consider how you will bring together the power of God and the Word of God through relational disciple-making.

 *Thought for Reflection*

Parents who have checked out must check back in!

Fresh Ideas

Read the "Fresh Ideas" and use one of them to assist you to become a bridge of influence to your kids. Place a ✔ by the one you choose and then record your thoughts on how you want to use it.

- Pick up a teen magazine at a newsstand, read it and make notes on what you observe.

- Go to the web site of the Center for Parent/Youth Understanding (www.cpyu.org) and read their reviews and updates on today's youth culture.

- Create a brainstorming discussion with your spouse and/or family on how the culture destroys young people, how parents abandon them, how the church struggles to relate to them, and yet how kids are searching for God.

- Take your kids to a bridge and explain to them your role in their lives as a bridge—connecting God to them and them to God. Then ask them to talk to you about how you can help them in that role. Ask what they need and want from you.

- Create a Bridge the Gap Profile. In it you can put items such as:

    - A description of the ways your kids buy into this disconnected generation.
    - A list of the ways you are disconnected from your kids.
    - A report on a conversation with your child on how he/she sees this generation as disconnected.
    - An account of a conversation with your child on how he/she sees himself/herself searching for God.

- When you see opportunities to connect with your kids, write them down, then follow through on some of them later.

- Jot down your thoughts about how to show your kids the power of God and the Word of God through meeting with them to pass on a passionate faith. Brainstorm ideas on how you can do that.

 Further Reading

Walt Mueller, The Center for Parent Youth Understanding, www.cpyu.org. This dynamic web site will offer you frequent updates on various elements of our culture that influence our kids.

PARENT FUEL JOURNAL

My Personal and Parenting Reflections

Use this space to record your insights, thoughts, emotions, hopes and dreams for yourself, your family and for each of your children.

For Myself:

For Our Family:

For My Children:

Burn Away the Junk to Find the Heart of Gold

How do we help our children discover their hearts?

PARENT FUEL JOURNAL

 Prayer to Begin

Lord Jesus, show me my heart and my children's hearts.

 Thought for Reflection

Parents to kids: from our hearts to their hearts!

 Quick Response

Briefly jot down your insights, thoughts and emotions after reading this chapter of the book.

 Verse to Memorize

Above all else, guard your heart, for it is the wellspring of life. (Proverbs 4:23)

My Daily Parenting Prayers

Pray one of these prayers each day and then write any other prayers or thoughts that the Lord brings to your mind.

Sunday

Guard of My Heart, show me how to guard my heart and how to teach my children to guard their hearts.

Monday

Light of the World, bring to light what is in my heart.

Tuesday

Purifier of All Hearts, show me what I need to remove from my heart.

Wednesday

Spring of Life, flood my heart with You! You are what I need to put in my heart.

Thursday

Revealer of All Truth, reveal to me how my children and I have bought into the Big Lie, the Bigger Lie and the Biggest Lie, and what to do about it.

Friday

River of Life, create a continual stream of Your life in my heart and in my children's hearts.

Saturday

Lord of All Relationships, connect my heart to my children's hearts.

PARENT FUEL JOURNAL

 Penetrating Questions

God wants you to know your heart and then to help your children know their hearts. Reflecting on these questions will guide you practically to discover your own heart and your children's hearts.

1. In the story I told about Ginny, to what aspect of the story did you relate in particular?

2. On a scale of 1-10 how well do you know your own heart? Your child's heart? Why did you give yourself that rating?

3. How would you describe one specific situation where you did not guard your heart and/or your child's heart?

4. Have you believed any or all of the lies discussed in this chapter? How do you need to *guard your heart* against these lies?

5. What do you need to do now to place a double-guard around your heart against the enemy without and the enemy within?

6. When you filled in the "My Heart" page, what did you deem most important about what you took out of your heart and about what you put in?

7. What specific change(s) do you need to make to stop responding to your kids' outward behavior and to start responding from your heart toward their hearts?

PARENT FUEL JOURNAL

 Taking Action

Focus on the "My Heart" page in the book. Answer the following:
1) What is in my heart?
2) What do I need to remove from my heart?
3) What do I need to put in my heart?

(Decide what you need from God so He can fill you from His source. These verses will get you started: Psalm 51:10-13; Psalm 119:11; Matthew 5:8; Romans 5:5; Galatians 5:22-23; Ephesians 5:18.)

From what you write, pick one heart issue and pursue it with God. (See Appendix 1 of *Parent Fuel* on page 247 for a more in-depth approach.)

 Thought for Reflection

From your heart and your children's hearts flows the Spring of Life!

 **Fresh Ideas**

Read the "Fresh Ideas" and use one of them to assist you to discover your own heart and your kids' hearts. Place a ✔ by the one you choose and then record your thoughts here on how you want to use it.

- Meet one-to-one with one of your children—just to let him or her talk and for you to listen.

- At a meal or family time read, discuss and memorize Proverbs 4:23.

- During a meal with your family present the Big, Bigger and Biggest Lies to your family. Talk about them. Look up the verses and discuss them. See if you can reach a conclusion about each lie.

- Watch this week to see where the enemy tries to invade you and your family.

- Create your own "Examine My Heart" retreat. Use this *Parent Fuel Journal* to guide you. During the retreat you can read the chapter again, then meditate on the John Eldredge quote on page 103 in the book. Spend time expanding on the "My Heart" page. Concentrate on Proverbs 4:23, and consider how it applies to you and to your family.

 Further Reading

Dave Busby, *The Heart of the Matter* (Minneapolis: Full Court Press, 1993). This dynamic video series will help your teenagers connect with their hearts. (Order from www.reach-out.org.)

John Flavel, *Keeping the Heart* (Morgan, PA: Soli Deo Gloria Publications, 1998). This classic book from the 1600s offers amazing insight into Proverbs 4:23 and the heart.

Gary Smalley, *The Key to Your Child's Heart* (Dallas: Word, 1992). This valuable resource from this renowned expert on love and relationships provides more insights on how parents connect to their kids' hearts.

PARENT FUEL JOURNAL

 My Personal and Parenting Reflections

Use this space to record your insights, thoughts, emotions, hopes and dreams for yourself, your family and for each of your children.

For Myself:

For Our Family:

For My Children:

Build a Fire that Blazes with Intimacy

How do we love our kids unconditionally?

Prayer to Begin

Lover of my Soul, thank You that Your love for me never ceases. Wherever I go, Your love pursues me. Whatever I do, Your love remains. Your love lives inside of me through Your Spirit. Please express Your love through me to each person in my family.

 Thought for Reflection

Love makes everything that is heavy light. (Thomas à Kempis)

 Quick Response

Briefly jot down your insights, thoughts and emotions from reading this chapter of the book.

 Verse to Memorize

...love in the Spirit. (Colossians 1:8)

My Daily Parenting Prayers

Pray one of these prayers each day and then write any other prayers or thoughts that the Lord brings to your mind.

Sunday

God of Love, build an environment of unconditional love in our home.

Monday

Lover of my Soul, give me Your love for each person in my family.

Tuesday

Spirit of Love, fill me with Your love so that I can love in the Spirit.

Wednesday

Creator of Marriage, give my spouse and me a strong and healthy marriage.

Thursday

Authority over all Authorities, build Your authority into our home and into my children. Let me love them enough to exercise Your authority with them.

Friday

Jesus, the Centerpiece of our Home, design our home so respect, obedience and honesty find a home in our children.

Saturday

Lord Jesus, use me to create intimacy in our home.

PARENT FUEL JOURNAL

 Penetrating Questions

Unconditional love comes only from God. Not only does God love you unconditionally, He wants to fill you with His love so you can love others that way. Reflecting on these questions will help you discover practically how to unconditionally love your family.

1. How has intimacy burned more brightly or diminished toward your spouse over the last few years?

2. What positive effect can *love in the Spirit* (Colossians 1:8) have on your spouse and children?

3. Knowing that the greatest thing you can do for your children is to love your spouse, what practical action will show your spouse that you love him/her unconditionally?

4. How do you see yourself growing in your marriage in the following areas (1 = the fire is out; 2 = the fire is still burning; 3 = the fire is hot)?
   - I accept my spouse without reservations or expectations.
   - I adapt to my spouse's desires.
   - I admire my spouse openly.
   - I appreciate my spouse by listening to him/her.
   - I act kindly toward my spouse.

5. How do you see yourself growing in your relationship to your children in these areas (1 = the fire is out; 2 = the fire is still burning; 3 = the fire is hot)?
   - I accept my children without reservations or expectations.
   - I adapt to my children's needs.
   - I admire my children openly.
   - I appreciate my children by listening to them.
   - I act kindly toward my children.

6. From looking at Ephesians 5:18 – 6:3 how has your view of your role in your family changed? Your spouse's role? Your children's?

7. What actions do you need to take to create an environment of obedience and respect with your kids?

PARENT FUEL JOURNAL

 Taking Action

With your spouse, draw a picture of a house with a foundation, frame and roof. Using what you discovered in this chapter of the book, determine how each one enhances and/or diminishes the intimacy in your family. Decide on one step of action to build intimacy in your home.

 Thought for Reflection

The greatest gift you can give your children is to love your spouse.

Build a Fire that Blazes with Intimacy

 Fresh Ideas

Read the "Fresh Ideas" and use one of them to assist you to go to a deeper level of intimacy in your home. Place a ✔ by the one you choose and then record your thoughts here on how you want to use it.

- If you struggle to love someone in your family, write out a prayer based on Romans 5:5 and Colossians 1:8. Daily pray that prayer for that person.

- With your spouse, read Ephesians 5:18-33. Write down how you view your role (not the role of the other person) and how you can carry out that role more effectively. Without trying to change the other person's viewpoint, communicate what you wrote with each other.

- Look at Ephesians 6:1-3 with your spouse. Write down your children's role in the family. Talk together about what you need to do to help your kids pursue that role.

- Attend a marriage retreat with your spouse to rekindle your intimacy.

 Further Reading

David and Teresa Ferguson, *Intimate Encounters*, www.greatcommandment.net. Both this workbook and the one following will give you more tools for developing intimacy in your family.

David and Teresa Ferguson, *Parenting with Intimacy*, www.greatcommandment.net.

PARENT FUEL JOURNAL

 My Personal and Parenting Reflections

Use this space to record your insights, thoughts, emotions, hopes and dreams for yourself, your family and for each of your children.

For Myself:

For Our Family:

For My Children:

Feed the Fire with Communication

How do we communicate positively with our kids?

Prayer to Begin

Lord of Love and Life... through the Cross, you prove Your love for me. Through the Resurrection, You provide Your life for me. Through the Holy Spirit living in me, You give me the power to love and communicate with my children.

 Thought for Reflection

Time given and attention focused lead to communication and closeness with our children.

 Quick Response

Briefly jot down your insights, thoughts and emotions from reading this chapter of the book.

 Verse to Memorize

...speak the truth in love. (Ephesians 4:15)

My Daily Parenting Prayers

Pray one of these prayers each day and then write any other prayers or thoughts that the Lord brings to your mind.

Sunday
God of Love, because of Your "in spite of" love in me I can love my children unconditionally and communicate with them positively.

Monday
Lord of my Time, give me discipline to change my schedule so my kids get time and focused attention.

Tuesday
Counselor, show me how to avoid or work through communication breakdowns in order not to stifle the flow of love.

Wednesday
Redeemer and Rescuer, when my kids go into the cave let me respond constructively to the messages coming out of the cave.

Thursday
Great Communicator, give me the awareness to remember and use Your communication skills.

Friday
Truth-Speaker, give me courage to speak the truth in love and create an environment of positive communication in our family.

Saturday
Lover of Our Family, work in each person in our family so that we listen to and talk to each other in ways that show Your love.

FUEL THE FIRE FIRST IN US

 Penetrating Questions

Loving communication with your children will take place only as the love of Jesus comes through you to your children. Reflecting on these questions will create a pathway for positive communication with your kids.

1. How did your parents communicate unconditional love to you, and how did that affect you? If they did not communicate unconditional love to you, how did that affect you?

2. Reflecting on Deuteronomy 6:7, what are you doing with your children to make liberal deposits of time and focused attention? What needs to change in your priorities and time schedule to make more deposits in them?

3. Specifically how do you withdraw love from your children's accounts? Give an example.

Feed the Fire with Communication

4. If your child/teenager has gone into the cave or will at some future time, what specific action do you need to take to work through or prepare for that experience?

5. What do you think the apostle Paul means when he uses the phrase *speaking the truth in love* (Ephesians 4:15)?

6. Of the seven communication skills, which one do you use best, and which one do you need the most? Why?

7. From your answer to #6, what specific action will you take to improve one communication skill with your children?

PARENT FUEL JOURNAL

 Taking Action

Ask your spouse and your children to give you honest feedback on how you communicate with your children. From that feedback consider three ways you can improve that communication. This week act on one improvement by building it into one activity that will give time and focused attention to your child.

 Thought for Reflection

Do your priorities and commitments reflect a child-focused home or a Christ-focused home?

Feed the Fire with Communication

 *Fresh Ideas*

Read the "Fresh Ideas" and use one of them to increase positive communication with your children. Place a ✔ by the one you choose and then record your thoughts here on how you want to use it.

- Following the outline of Deuteronomy 6:7, design your plan for making positive, daily deposits of unconditional love in your children.

- Analyze your Unconditional Love Account by reviewing your deposits and withdrawals for each of your children. Create two columns labeled Deposits and Withdrawals, listing positive and negative communications with examples. Reconcile your account by deciding how to improve communication with your children and then acting on what you decide.

- Using the seven communication skills, write down one check you want to write to each of your children. Give each one his or her check!

- Make a large deposit by planning a special one-on-one time with one of your children this week. Think creatively about an activity that he or she would enjoy, and then do it. Each week do the same until you have had one-on-one time with each child. Consider continuing this on a weekly basis.

 Further Reading

Ross Campbell, *How to Really Love Your Child* and *How to Really Love Your Teenager* (Colorado Springs: Cook Communications, revised editions 2004). These books have been around a long time. That's because they express the timeless truth that loving our kids with God's love is the basis of everything else that parents do.

PARENT FUEL JOURNAL

 My Personal and Parenting Reflections

Use this space to record your insights, thoughts, emotions, hopes and dreams for yourself, your family and for each of your children.

For Myself:

For Our Family:

For My Children:

Pour Fuel on the Fire by Making Disciples

How do we invest in Jesus-focused relationships with our kids and their friends?

PARENT FUEL JOURNAL

 Prayer to Begin

Greatest of All Disciple-makers, show me how to disciple my kids and their friends.

 Thought for Reflection

When we stand before Jesus and the important issues of life become clearer than we have ever seen them before, what will be truly important? Surely those of us who know Jesus will hold out to Him our relationship with Him and our investment in other people, particularly our family and our children.

 Quick Response

Briefly jot down your insights, thoughts and emotions after reading this chapter of the book.

 Verse to Memorize

For what is our hope, our joy, or the crown in which we will glory in the presence of our Lord Jesus when he comes? Is it not you? Indeed, you are our glory and joy. (1 Thessalonians 2:19)

My Daily Parenting Prayers

Pray one of these prayers each day and then write any other prayers or thoughts that the Lord brings to your mind.

Sunday
God Who is Always Worthy, lead me to live a life worthy of You before my family.

Monday
Jesus in Whose Name I Pray, give me the discipline to go "To My Knees" to pray daily for my children.

Tuesday
Jesus Who Answers Prayers, daily remind me of John Bunyan's words: "You can do more than pray after you have prayed, but you cannot do more than pray until you have prayed."

Wednesday
Counselor Who Connects All Relationships, show me how to get "In Their Lives" so I can respond to the teachable moments and build strong relationships with my kids.

Thursday
Counselor, Who Breaks Down All Relational Barriers, daily remind me of the words of Thomas Merton: "In the end it is personal relationships that save everything."

Friday
Great Discipler, give me courage to create a platform to formally disciple my kids and their friends "Toward Their Maturity."

Saturday
Author of The Great Commission, daily remind me of this reality: "Reproducing disciples by multiplication is God's way of fulfilling the Great Commission!"

Penetrating Questions

A significant opportunity lies before you to invest in a Jesus-focused relationship with your kids and their friends. Reflecting on these questions will help you discover practically how to pursue that investment.

1. Reflecting on 1 Thessalonians 2:19, do you view your kids and their friends as a long-term investment? Make a list of the potential dividends.

2. Understanding from 1 Thessalonians 1:2-3 that you must make the "To My Knees" investment first, what specific actions will you take to deepen your own prayer life and to pray for your kids and their friends?

3. Meditating on 1 Thessalonians 2:8, how do you relate that verse to your kids and their friends? What specific *informal discipleship* actions do you need to take to get "In Their Lives?"

4. Considering the word *urging* in 1 Thessalonians 2:11-12, how do you understand your role of having spiritual authority to urge your kids to experience life-change and become life-changers?

5. Reviewing the "Toward Their Maturity" ideas built on 1 Thessalonians 2:13 and 2 Timothy 2:1-2, what platform will you build to *formally disciple* your kids and their friends? Be specific.

6. What five practical steps will you take to begin a discipleship group with your kids and their friends? (Use "The Practical Steps to Discipling Your Kids and Their Friends" in Appendix 3 of *Parent Fuel* on pages 253-256 as a guide.)

7. In one sentence what is your vision for making disciples of your kids and their friends?

Taking Action

Prayerfully consider this once-in-a-lifetime investment opportunity to disciple your kids and your kids' friends, then make a decision about pursuing it. If you decide to go for it, write out a one-page Plan of Action with the steps you will take to make this a reality. (To guide you, read through "The Practical Steps to Discipling Your Kids and Their Friends" in Appendix 3 of *Parent Fuel* on pages 253 – 256.)

 Thought for Reflection

You can equip your kids to experience life change and to become life-changers.

 ## *Fresh Ideas*

Read the "Fresh Ideas" and choose one of them to assist you in making a Jesus-focused investment in your kids and their friends. Place a ✔ by the one you choose and then record your thoughts here on how you want to use it.

- Using the phrases of 1 Thessalonians 2:19, close your eyes and picture your kids. Let God speak to you as you imagine what they will be like in ten years and in eternity.

- Begin your day by going "To My Knees" in prayer for your children. Decide what specific forms that prayer will take.

- Take specific action this week to get "In Their Lives." Consider taking each child out this week just to talk—asking questions and actively listening.

- Move toward your kids rather than away from them by inviting their friends to your home to feed them.

- Design your specific plan for moving your kids "Toward Their Maturity" by making disciples of your kids and their friends. Write out specific, practical steps with details, using what you discovered in this chapter. (See "The Practical Steps to Discipling Your Kids and Their Friends" in Appendix 3 of *Parent Fuel* on pages 253-256 as a guide.)

 ## *Further Reading*

Robert Coleman, *The Master Plan of Evangelism* (Grand Rapids, MI: Fleming H. Revell, 1963). This classic text will show you the specific plan Jesus followed to develop His disciples.

Leroy Eims, *The Lost Art of Disciple Making* (Grand Rapids, MI: Zondervan, 1978). This masterpiece will give you practical, biblical instruction on how to disciple another person.

PARENT FUEL JOURNAL

My Personal and Parenting Reflections

Use this space to record your insights, thoughts, emotions, hopes and dreams for yourself, your family and for each of your children.

For Myself:

For Our Family:

For My Children:

Fan the Flame with Discipline

How do we equip our children to move from dependence to independence?

PARENT FUEL JOURNAL

 Prayer to Begin

God of discipline, thank You that You love me enough to discipline me. And You do it for my good that I may share in Your holiness. Jesus, full of grace, give me Your ability to discipline my children with grace, not rules. Spirit of freedom, free me and my children to move from dependence to independence. Spirit of wisdom, fill me with Your wisdom to apply discipline daily with grace and toward freedom.

 Thought for Reflection

Discipline is the tool by which God measures desires.

 Quick Response

Briefly jot down your insights, thoughts and emotions from reading this chapter in the book.

 Verse to Memorize

Our fathers disciplined us for a little while as they thought best; but God disciplines us for our good, that we may share in his holiness. (Hebrews 12:10)

My Daily Parenting Prayers

Pray one of these prayers each day and then write any other prayers or thoughts that the Lord brings to your mind.

Sunday
Father, thank You that out of Your fatherly love for me You discipline me.

Monday
Father of discipline, give me grace to receive Your discipline and to exercise discipline in my own life. Please let that be a positive example of discipline to my children.

Tuesday
Graceful God, give me grace to avoid legalistic rules and to offer my children Your graceful discipline.

Wednesday
God of wisdom, by Your Spirit help me to know how to apply discipline to my children each day.

Thursday
God of insight, show me one issue on which I need to focus in order to apply discipline in my child's life. Show me how to design my plan of action and carry it out consistently.

Friday
Father of discipline, bring a "harvest of righteousness and peace" (Hebrews 12:11) through the way I discipline my children.

Saturday
Father of freedom, please move my children from dependence to independence.

Penetrating Questions

Moving your children from dependence to independence takes biblical discipline in the context of grace. Reflecting on these questions will help you listen to God as He shows you His unique approach to disciplining each of your children.

1. How would you describe your approach to handling your children now—punishment, permissiveness or discipline?

2. Do you make decisions about your children from fear? If so, how do you think that affects your child? (Discuss this question with your spouse.)

3. In conversation with your spouse, specifically what do you need to do to change your disciplinary approach?

4. From what you discovered in this chapter, how do you define discipline? What purpose and goal does discipline have, and how will you pursue it?

5. What one discipline issue in your family would you describe as hot right now? Why?

6. What will you do to address that issue from what you learned in this chapter?

7. How do you think disciple-making with your kids and their friends can help you discipline your teenager?

PARENT FUEL JOURNAL

 Taking Action

Determine one issue where discipline is needed with your child. Applying what you learned in this chapter, design a plan to address that issue. Begin by writing your definition of and guidelines for discipline, then draw up a specific agreement and discuss it with your child.

 Thought for Reflection

Discipline: external control that, when removed, leads to internal self-control.

Fresh Ideas

Read the "Fresh Ideas" and choose one of them to assist you in disciplining your children. Place a ✔ by the one you choose and then record your thoughts here on how you want to use it.

- Put the foundation under discipline by discipling your teenager *before* implementing a plan of discipline. Follow through on Chapter 10 *before* trying to apply this chapter. In the context of disciple-making our kids will move down the road of discipline much more quickly!

- When it appears that your child does something wrong, discern the real issue before passing judgment. This will help you apply discipline much more accurately.

- Write down all the rules your family has now, ask yourself why you have them and see how many you can eliminate.

- Think of several low-risk decisions that you make for your kids now. Decide to turn the decision-making process toward them, and say, "You decide."

- Join a group of parents at your church who have children your age. Engage in conversation about how you will discipline your children.

 ## *Further Reading*

James Dobson, *The New Dare to Discipline* (Wheaton, IL: Tyndale House, 1996). As the foremost authority on family and children, James Dobson provides penetrating and powerful insights into how to discipline our children.

PARENT FUEL JOURNAL

My Personal and Parenting Reflections

Use this space to record your insights, thoughts, emotions, hopes and dreams for yourself, your family and for each of your children.

For Myself:

For Our Family:

For My Children:

Intensify the Heat with Destiny

How do we inspire our kids to discover their unique direction in life?

Prayer to Begin

God of all Destinies, You placed my family's destiny "in Christ". As we pursue You, reveal Your destiny for each of us. Help my children and me answer life's big questions: *Who am I? Where am I going? How am I going to get there?*

 ## Thought for Reflection

With great delight God eagerly wants to show you your identity that leads to your destiny.

 ## Quick Response

Briefly jot down your insights, thoughts and emotions after reading this chapter of the book.

 ## Verse to Memorize

It is in Christ that we find out who we are and what we are living for. (Ephesians 1:11, The Message)

My Daily Parenting Prayers

Pray one of these prayers each day and then write any other prayers or thoughts that the Lord brings to your mind.

Sunday

Lord Jesus, show my children and me the answers to *Who am I? Where am I going? And how am I going to get there?*

Monday

Christ, who lives in me, let my children and me see more clearly the answer to the question, *Who am I in Christ?* (Ephesians 1:1-14)

Tuesday

Holy Spirit, who guides our destinies, lead my children and me to answer the question, *Where am I going?*

Wednesday

Light of the World, send forth Your light to my children and me. Let Your light shine on us so we can answer the question, *How am I going to get there?*

Thursday

God, whose name I praise, allow my children and me to discover how to live to reflect Your glory (Ephesians 1:6, 12, 14).

Friday

Jesus, who chose us in You before the foundation of the world, guide my children and me through the nine destiny deciders so we can know Your specific destiny for our lives.

Saturday

God, who brings glory to Yourself, let us live out our destinies to reflect Your glory.

PARENT FUEL JOURNAL

❓ *Penetrating Questions*

Working with your children to discover their destinies takes time and focus. Concentrating on these questions will lead you toward a specific approach.

1. If one of your children asks you to answer the *Who am I?* question, what will you say?

2. If one of your children asks you to answer the *Where am I going?* question, how will you answer?

3. If one of your children asks you the *How am I going to get there?* question, what response will you give?

4. How will you explain to your children what it means for their destiny to be *in Christ?*

5. How will you communicate to your kids their clear-cut destination: to live to reflect God's glory?

6. Of the nine destiny-deciders, on which ones do you need to work yourself in order to teach them to your children?

7. What decisions do you need to make now in order to lead your children through the nine destiny-deciders over time?

PARENT FUEL JOURNAL

 Taking Action

Write out your plan to answer the questions *Who am I? Where am I going? How am I going to get there?* with your kids. Realizing that this is a long-term project, map this out over time, deciding when, where, and how you will pursue it. Then take one small step to start.

 *Thought for Reflection*

What is your dash?

 *Fresh Ideas*

Read the "Fresh Ideas" and choose one of them to assist you in helping your kids discover their destiny. Place a ✔ by the one you choose and then record your thoughts here on how you want to use it.

- Consider how to work through the information in this chapter as a long-term rather than a short-term project.

- Think about the age at which discussions about these issues will be meaningful for your kids. Then put a time frame on when you will pursue this before they graduate from high school.

- If you think your kids can handle these discussions now, decide when you will set up weekly conversations with your kids about these topics. Use this as an opportunity for long-term discipleship with your kids and their friends. Decide on a fun activity each week that will go along with your serious discussions. Determine the material you need by looking at the list in this chapter, and then order it from www.reach-out.org.

- Meet with a group of parents regularly to discuss how you can support each other in discipling your children.

 Further Reading

Watchman Nee, *Sit, Walk, Stand* (Wheaton, IL: Tyndale House, 1977). This wonderful little volume on Ephesians will take you deeper into answering the three questions we addressed in this chapter.

PARENT FUEL JOURNAL

My Personal and Parenting Reflections

Use this space to record your insights, thoughts, emotions, hopes and dreams for yourself, your family and for each of your children.

For Myself:

For Our Family:

For My Children:

Don't Let Disappointment Douse the Fire

How do we build our children's confidence in God when life lets them down?

PARENT FUEL JOURNAL

 Prayer to Begin

Great God, You are always in control of every circumstance—even when I don't understand it. I acknowledge that everything filters through Your good hand before it gets to me.

 Thought for Reflection

Our greatest success comes after our biggest disappointments. (Henry Ward Beecher)

 Quick Response

Briefly jot down your insights, thoughts and emotions after reading this chapter of the book.

 Verse to Memorize

I will extol the Lord at all times; his praise will always be on my lips. My soul will boast in the Lord; let the afflicted hear and rejoice. Glorify the Lord with me; let us exalt his name together. (Psalm 34:1-3)

My Daily Parenting Prayers

Pray one of these prayers each day and then write any other prayers or thoughts that the Lord brings to your mind.

Sunday

Great God, You are great and greatly to be praised. You are greater than my circumstances. Give our family a greater desire to praise You.

Monday

Good God, You are good and Your goodness endures forever. You are good no matter how bad my life situation is. Let our family see You in the good and the bad situations.

Tuesday

God Over the Good and Bad, I desire to look for You and call on You in the good and bad times of my life. Take my family and me on a God Hunt.

Wednesday

Elohim—The True and Mighty God, who sees all problems, I choose to *gaze* at You and *glance* at my problems. Help our family make that our motto.

Thursday

Jehovah—Present to Meet Every Need, meet the needs of our family.

Friday

Adonai—The Lord Who Rules and Reigns, I choose to submit myself and my family to You and Your work in our lives.

Saturday

Lord, lead my family and me to "taste" You, "take refuge" in You and "fear" You, then we will "lack nothing." (Psalm 34:8-9)

PARENT FUEL JOURNAL

 Penetrating Questions

Teaching your children how to turn to God when "the bottom drops out" presents one of life's biggest challenges to parents. Hopefully answering these questions will give you direction for that challenge.

1. In what way has the bottom dropped out for you and/or for each of your children?

2. Reflecting on John 16:33, Romans 8:28-29 and the Alan Redpath poem on page 205 in the book, how do you need to adjust your view of your life as it relates to suffering? What do you think God is doing through the difficulties you and your children face right now?

3. Considering what David went through that got him "nailed to the wall" (1 Samuel 18-24), how do you and your children identify with his difficulties? In the past how have you tried to solve your difficult situations?

4. Do you feel you've ever been nailed to the wall in the back of a cave with no place to turn but to God? If so, how? Did you or will you, like David, decide to go on a God Hunt?

5. On your God Hunt how will you and your kids *gaze* instead of *glance* at the power of *Elohim—The True and Mighty God?* What one specific action will you take to trust His power as you face your difficulties?

6. On your God Hunt how will you and your kids *gaze* instead of *glance* at the presence of *Jehovah—Present to Meet Every Need?* What one specific action will you take to pursue His presence in the midst of your problems?

7. On your God Hunt how will you and your kids *gaze* instead of *glance* at the authority of *Adonai—The Lord Who Rules and Reigns?* What one specific action will you take to release control to His authority in the midst of your struggles?

PARENT FUEL JOURNAL

 Taking Action

Go on a God Hunt. Identify the most difficult experience your child faces. Find out when the bottom dropped out, where he or she got nailed to the wall, and how he or she perceived God in light of this situation. Talk this through in several one-on-one conversations asking variations of the question, "Where do you see God working in this situation?" Then, using the information you learned in this chapter, discuss what he/she needs in order to *glance* at the problem and *gaze* at God.

 ***Thought for Reflection***

Glance at the problem and *gaze* at God.

Fresh Ideas

Read the "Fresh Ideas" and choose one of them to help you go on a God Hunt. Place a ✔ by the one you choose and then record your thoughts here on how you want to use it.

- Begin the habit of journaling the God Hunt insights you discover with your kids. Later the journal will serve as a positive confidence-builder as you look back on how God has worked through various difficulties.

- Buy several CDs of praise music. Play them at home and in the car. If you have teenagers, buy the ones they prefer. After a song or two go on a God Hunt, asking your kids to recount one thing they learned about God from the song.

- Gather for a God Hunt Family Night regularly. Together memorize one verse each week of Psalm 34:1-9. Share personal insights on how you see God working through the difficulties.

 Further Reading

Philip Yancey, *Where Is God When It Hurts?* (Grand Rapids, MI: Zondervan, 1990). This penetrating volume explains the role God plays in human suffering.

PARENT FUEL JOURNAL

My Personal and Parenting Reflections

Use this space to record your insights, thoughts, emotions, hopes and dreams for yourself, your family and for each of your children.

For Myself:

For Our Family:

For My Children:

Glow in the Light of God's Vision

How do we motivate our kids to pursue God's dream for their lives?

Prayer to Begin

King of Kings, lead our family to seek Your Kingdom dreams instead of our own.

 Thought for Reflection

Measure success not by self-gratification, but by self-sacrifice.

 Quick Response

Briefly jot down your insights, thoughts and emotions after reading this chapter of the book.

 Verse to Memorize

But seek first his kingdom and his righteousness, and all these things will be given to you as well. (Matthew 6:33)

My Daily Parenting Prayers

Pray one of these prayers each day and then write any other prayers or thoughts that the Lord brings to your mind.

Sunday

God Who Sees All Things, show me the places where I cause my family to have blurred vision.

Monday

Lord Who Creates Vision, lead our family toward 20/20 vision of You.

Tuesday

God of Glory, I desire for my vision and the vision of my family to be focused on glorifying You by finding our satisfaction in You.

Wednesday

Lord of My Life, may my vision of glorifying You by finding my satisfaction in You drive every personal and family decision I make.

Thursday

God Who Knows Your Will for My Life, allow me to understand Your vision and participate in Your Vision Design for my life and for my children's lives.

Friday

Light of the World, give me insight and courage to implement at least one of Your four models of ministry. Please use that effort to increase my kids' vision of You.

Saturday

Lord of My Life and Family, cause me to always answer positively: Am I willing to do whatever it takes to let You use my children's lives for Your glory?

Penetrating Questions

Naturally you want to hold on to your children, rather than release them. You probably find it difficult to die to your own dreams for your children and to live for God's dreams for them. These questions will guide you in the process of releasing them to God.

1. How would you express the difference between the American Dream and the Kingdom Dream? Be specific.

2. How do you think God wants to use your life to change the world for His glory?

3. After answering the three "eye exam" questions on page 220 in the book, how do your intentions line up with God's desires for your kids? Can you say that you are totally motivated toward God's vision for your life? For your children's lives?

4. In what ways does the vision statement *to glorify God by finding our satisfaction in Him* express or not express your personal vision?

5. How has the "The Vision Design" process worked out in your life? Your kids' lives?

6. Which of the four models do you think will increase the vision of your family? Why?

7. From the model you picked, what specific plans do you have to implement it?

Taking Action

Select one of the four ministry models, and put that model into action. Make your selection according to which one you think will increase the Kingdom Dream vision in your family.

 ## Thought for Reflection

The American Dream of *getting* pales in comparison to the Kingdom Dream of *giving*.

Glow in the Light of God's Vision

 Fresh Ideas

Read the "Fresh Ideas" and choose one of them to assist you in motivating your kids toward God's vision for their lives. Place a ✔ by the one you choose and then record your thoughts here on how you want to use it.

- Draw up a contract like the one Bill and Vonette Bright wrote, expressing your desire to become a slave of Jesus Christ. Include some of the ideas from this chapter in that contract.

- Think about how you can enjoy God more. Write a paragraph, song, or other creative expression to God that conveys your enjoyment of Him.

- Involve your family in a body of believers where the worship is alive, Jesus and the Bible are talked about warmly, and ministry, not entertainment, guides the youth group. Even if it means changing churches, place your family in a healthy spiritual environment. Look for a way to get involved in the youth ministry and for places where your kids can deepen their understanding of God's vision for them.

- Consider taking some training to develop your ability to minister to others and to share your faith. Teach your children what you learn, and then practice it together.

- Write a one-sentence prayer asking God to accomplish His vision for your children's lives. Record the prayer on a card, and put it in a place that will remind you to pray it daily.

 Further Reading

John Piper, *Desiring God* (Portland: Multnomah Press, 1986, revised and expanded edition 2003). This powerful book provides an in-depth study of what it means to glorify God.

Barry St. Clair, *Giving Away Your Faith*, Reach Out Youth Solutions. This practical book will help you develop the "telling" model. It guides kids on the wild adventure of overcoming their fears and taking the risk to boldly communicate Christ.

Barry St. Clair, *Influencing Your World*, Reach Out Youth Solutions. This book will help you and your kids develop the models of loving, serving, and caring. Through it your kids will grow as influential leaders through serving the needs of people around them.

PARENT FUEL JOURNAL

My Personal and Parenting Reflections

Use this space to record your insights, thoughts, emotions, hopes and dreams for yourself, your family and for each of your children.

For Myself:

For Our Family:

For My Children:

Spread the Fire of God's Desire

How do we release our children to change the world?

Prayer to Begin

Compassionate Lord, give our family Your vision for the world and Your love for people. Jesus, Who Desires That None Should Perish, fill my children and me with a burden to tell two or three people around us about You. Lord Over All the Nations, touch my children's hearts and call them to reach the world.

 Thought for Reflection

God desires to use your children to finish fulfilling the Great Commision.

 Quick Response

Briefly jot down your insights, thoughts and emotions after reading this chapter of the book.

 Verse to Memorize

Then Jesus came to them and said, "All authority in heaven and on earth has been given to me. Therefore, go and make disciples of all nations…" (Matthew 28:18-19)

My Daily Parenting Prayers

Pray one of these prayers each day and then write any other prayers or thoughts that the Lord brings to your mind.

Sunday
God of Abraham, You have blessed my family and me. Show us how to use these blessings to bless others.

Monday
God of Courage and Obedience, give me courage and obedience to give my children completely to You.

Tuesday
God Who Says "Go," reveal to my family and me Your vision for us to "Go into all the world and make disciples…"

Wednesday
Holy Spirit, provide my family and me with Your power to be Your witnesses to the people around us everywhere we go.

Thursday
Jesus, open the door for our family to take a Great Commission trip.

Friday
God of the Next Generation, use my children beyond their wildest imagination to change their generation.

Saturday
God Who Loves the World, touch my children's hearts and call them to take the message of Jesus to the world.

PARENT FUEL JOURNAL

 Penetrating Questions

Expanding your children's vision of the world and teaching them to see how God wants to use them challenges your faith to the max. Specifically answering these questions will assist you in meeting that challenge.

1. How did you rate yourself on the "Get Out of the House/Freak Out Survey?"

2. Do you think that God put you on this earth so you can *be blessed to be a blessing?* Why or why not?

3. What does the story of Abraham releasing his son Isaac to God mean to you as it relates to your releasing your children to God?

4. When you hear statistics and stories about the Holy Spirit's activity around the world, how do you respond? Why?

5. How do you react when you read the Great Commission in Matthew 28:18-20? How do you relate it to yourself? To your kids?

6. How can you help your kids break out of their own little worlds? What does your family's Acts 1:8 Strategy look like?

7. What benefits do you see for yourself, your family and your children by implementing your Acts 1:8 Strategy?

PARENT FUEL JOURNAL

 Taking Action

Make the decision to release your children to change the world. Then, using what you learned in this chapter, map out your route to get out of the house, catch a glimpse of the world, join the mission, and take a trip—a detailed Acts 1:8 Strategy.

 ***Thought for Reflection***

Get out of the house!

 ## Fresh Ideas

Read the "Fresh Ideas" and choose one of them to assist you in releasing your children to change the world. Place a ✔ by the one you choose and then record your thoughts here on how you want to use it.

- Place this prayer where you will be reminded to pray it often: "Lord, I release my children to you. Use them to change the world."

- With your spouse draw two pictures. (No artistic skills needed.) 1: Your expectations of your children's future. 2: God's desires for your children's future. Frankly discuss how those two pictures differ. Then write a one-paragraph reflection on why you find it hard to release your children to God and what steps you will take to release them to Him.

- With your family read Genesis 12: 1-3, then brainstorm a list of at least ten ways God has blessed you. Next make a list of ten ways you can bless others. Do this often with your family.

- Sit in your children's rooms for thirty minutes each, looking at what you see there. Make a list of what appears to be important to them. Of those things, what hinders each one from following Jesus? What encourages him/her to follow Jesus?

- In conversation with your child, choose one friend who needs Jesus. Use one or all four of Jesus' models to love, serve, care for and tell that friend.

- Plan a night to write your testimonies as a family and share them with each other.

- With your child, pray about and plan a missions trip you will take together in the next year.

- Read out loud a missionary book with your family at the evening meal, before bed, traveling in the car, or on vacation. I recommend the movie/book combination of *End of the Spear* and *Through Gates of Splendor* by Elisabeth Elliot. The movie and the documentary tell the powerful story of five missionaries martyred by the Auca Indians in 1956.

Further Reading

Patrick Johnstone, *Operation World* (Grand Rapids, MI: Zondervan, 2001); www.gmi.org/ow. This book provides a compilation of information on each country in the world and how to pray for each country.

John Piper, *Let the Nations Be Glad* (Grand Rapids, MI: Baker, 2003). This popular volume gives a challenge to pursue God's missionary plan for the world.

Barry St. Clair, *Leading Edge Climber's Guide*, Reach Out Youth Solutions. This training manual equips your kids for a cross-cultural trip. Focusing on seven leadership qualities of Jesus, it prepares your kids to discover these seven qualities of Jesus and then apply them on a mission trip.

Spread the Fire of God's Desire

 ## My Personal and Parenting Reflections

Use this space to record your insights, thoughts, emotions, hopes and dreams for yourself, your family and for each of your children.

For Myself:

For Our Family:

For My Children:

PARENT FUEL JOURNAL

Parent Fuel Journaling Pages

The blank pages provided in this Journal have very specific purposes. You can use them either to journal your discoveries as you go through *Parent Fuel* and *Parent Fuel Journal* or to journal after you complete the *Parent Fuel* book and journal.

This legend may help you to organize and categorize your thoughts. Using the initials below you can mark to whom your insights apply.

- P—Personal—for your own personal insights
- S—Spouse—for insights about your spouse
- F—Family—for insights about your entire family
- C—Children—for insights about your children (Adapt this using each child's initials.)

The journal you keep will become a treasure for you and your family both now and in the years to come.

Journaling Pages

PARENT FUEL JOURNAL

Journaling Pages

PARENT FUEL JOURNAL

Journaling Pages

PARENT FUEL JOURNAL

Journaling Pages

PARENT FUEL JOURNAL

Journaling Pages

PARENT FUEL JOURNAL

Journaling Pages

PARENT FUEL JOURNAL

Journaling Pages

PARENT FUEL JOURNAL

PARENT FUEL JOURNAL

Journaling Pages

PARENT FUEL JOURNAL

Journaling Pages

PARENT FUEL JOURNAL

Journaling Pages

PARENT FUEL JOURNAL

Journaling Pages

PARENT FUEL JOURNAL

Journaling Pages

PARENT FUEL JOURNAL

Journaling Pages

PARENT FUEL JOURNAL

Journaling Pages

PARENT FUEL JOURNAL

Journaling Pages

PARENT FUEL JOURNAL

Journaling Pages

PARENT FUEL JOURNAL

Journaling Pages

PARENT FUEL JOURNAL

Journaling Pages

PARENT FUEL JOURNAL

Journaling Pages

PARENT FUEL JOURNAL

Journaling Pages

PARENT FUEL JOURNAL

Journaling Pages

PARENT FUEL JOURNAL

Journaling Pages

PARENT FUEL JOURNAL

Journaling Pages